GEO

MW01130617

WHY ANIMALS LOOK DIFFERENT

Animal Skin and Fur

Jonatha A. Brown

Reading consultant: Susan Nations, M.Ed., author/literacy coach/
consultant in literacy development
Science and curriculum consultant: Debra Voege, M.A., science
and math curriculum resource teacher

Please visit our web site at: www.garethstevens.com
For a free color catalog describing Weekly Reader® Early Learning Library's list
of high-quality books, call 1-877-445-5824 (USA) or 1-800-387-3178 (Canada).
Weekly Reader® Early Learning Library's fax: (414) 336-0164.

Library of Congress Cataloging-in-Publication Data

Brown, Jonatha A.
   Animal skin and fur / by Jonatha A. Brown.
     p. cm. — (Why animals look different)
   Includes bibliographical references and index.
   ISBN-10: 0-8368-6862-5 – ISBN-13: 978-0-8368-6862-3 (lib. bdg.)
   ISBN-10: 0-8368-6867-6 – ISBN-13: 978-0-8368-6867-8 (softcover)
   1. Skin—Juvenile literature. 2. Fur—Juvenile literature. I. Title.
  II. Series: Brown, Jonatha A. Why animals look different.
  QL941B76 2007
  573.5'33—dc22
                           2006010999

This edition first published in 2007 by
Weekly Reader® Early Learning Library
A Member of the WRC Media Family of Companies
330 West Olive Street, Suite 100
Milwaukee, WI 53212 USA

Copyright © 2007 by Weekly Reader® Early Learning Library

Editor: Gini Holland
Art direction: Tammy West
Cover design and page layout: Charlie Dahl
Picture research: Diane Laska-Swanke

Picture credits: Cover, title, © Angela Scott/naturepl.com; pp. 4, 6, 11, 18, 19 © Michael H. Francis;
p. 5 © James P. Rowan; p. 7 © Bob Newman/Visuals Unlimited; pp. 8, 10, 14 © Tom and Pat Leeson;
p. 9 © Anup Shah/naturepl.com; p. 12 © Jose B. Ruiz/naturepl.com; p. 13 © Joe McDonald/Visuals
Unlimited; p. 15 © Dave Watts/naturepl.com; p. 16 © Doc White/naturepl.com; p. 17 © Gerald & Buff
Corsi/Visuals Unlimited; p. 20 © Benjam Pontinen/naturepl.com; p. 21 © Jim Merli/Visuals Unlimited

Printed in the United States of America

1 2 3 4 5 6 7 8 9 10 09 08 07 06

Table of Contents

Cover and title page: The cheetah has a spotted coat. The spots help hide the cheetah in tall grass while it hunts its prey.

A thick coat of fur helps keep these buffaloes warm in the winter.

Cover Up!

Skin and fur help animals in many ways. The buffalo's **thick** fur coat helps it stay warm. The porcupine's sharp **spines** help protect it from attack. A lizard's thick skin keeps it from drying out in the desert.

The giraffe has brown spots on its fur. These spots help a giraffe hide among trees as it feeds on leaves.

Each kind of animal has the skin or fur it needs. Skin and fur help the animal stay alive in the place where it lives.

This giraffe is hard to see among the trees. This animal's spotted coat helps it hide.

Polar bears have thick fur that is almost white. Thick fur keeps the bear warm.

Keeping Warm, Keeping Cool

Many animals that live in cold places have thick fur to keep them warm. The polar bear's fur looks white, but it is almost **clear**. Sunlight passes through it and warms the bear's skin. Then the bear's thick fur holds this heat in.

Camels live in the desert, where it is cold at night and hot during the day. They stay warm at night because their long, thick fur keeps heat in. During the day, this fur keeps some of the sun's heat out.

The camel's fur helps it stay both warm and cool.

This Arctic fox has a thin coat in the warm months. Its coat will be much thicker in the winter.

The Arctic fox has a thick winter coat. It sheds this coat in the spring, and a thinner coat grows in. The thin coat helps the fox keep cool in summer. The fox sheds its thin coat in the fall, and its warm winter coat grows back.

Hiding

Some animals have fur or skin that helps them hide among plants or rocks. Coloring that helps an animal hide is called **camouflage**. A tiger's stripes are a kind of camouflage. They make the tiger hard to see in tall grass.

A striped coat helps this tiger hide in tall grass. Hiding in the grass helps it sneak up on its prey.

This antelope is hard to see. Its tan fur helps it hide in the desert.

Antelopes have tan fur that helps them hide in the sandy desert. Lions have tan fur, too. The color tan makes the lion hard to see in dry grasses and bushes. A polar bear's nearly white fur is hard to see against snow and ice.

The fur of some animals changes color with the **seasons**. In the fall, the snowshoe hare grows a white coat. White fur makes the hare hard to see in the snow. In the spring, the hare sheds its white fur. The hare grows a brown coat for summer. Now it can hide in the dry, brown summer grass.

A snowshoe hare hides behind a bush on a summer day. Its brown coat is almost the same color as the ground and the dry twigs.

This octopus lives in the ocean. It changes colors as it crawls over rocks and plants on the bottom of the ocean.

Some animals change color as they move from place to place. The skin of an octopus can change color! It can turn brown, green, dark red, and black. Color changes help the octopus hide among rocks in the ocean.

Protection

Fur and skin can also **protect** animals. Male lions have thick, furry manes that make them look big and tough. A big mane can scare away other male lions. A thick mane also protects the lion's neck in a fight.

This male lion has a thick, furry mane. This mane may keep the lion from being bitten on the throat during a fight.

A porcupine's fur is full of long, sharp quills. These quills help keep the porcupine safe from enemies.

Porcupines have sharp **quills** in their fur. When an enemy attacks a porcupine, the porcupine tries to stick quills into its **enemy**. Quills hurt a lot. Most animals try to stay away from prickly porcupines.

Frilled lizards have a large flap of skin around their necks. When they are scared, they spread the flap open so that it forms a big frill. Now the lizard looks like a dragon! This helps the lizard scare enemies away.

This frilled lizard spreads its frill to look big and scary.

Thick fur keeps water away from an otter's skin. This helps the otter stay warm and dry in cold water.

Staying Dry

Beavers spend lots of time in water, but they need to keep their skin dry and warm. They have very thick coats that water cannot soak through. The sea otter has even thicker fur. When an otter comes out of the water, a quick shake leaves it nearly dry.

Penguins have to swim in icy water to hunt for food. These birds have very greasy feathers that keep water off their skin. Their feather coats are also very thick. These thick coats help penguins stay warm when they dive and swim.

These penguins are diving into icy cold water. Their thick coats of greasy feathers will keep them warm and dry.

This salamander has thin skin. It can soak up water right through this thin skin.

Staying Moist

Salamanders and most frogs have very thin skin. Their skin is so thin that they can lie in a puddle and soak up water through it. Thin skin also dries out quickly. For this reason, most frogs can live only in damp places.

Some tree frogs can live in dry places. They have very thick skin that helps keep water in. Lizards and snakes have thick skin, too. It keeps their bodies from drying out, the same way the tree frog's skin does.

This horned lizard lives in the desert. Its thick skin helps keep the lizard from drying out.

Wide flaps of skin allow this flying squirrel to glide like a kite! It cannot fly, but it can glide far.

Strange but True!

The gliding squirrel has flaps of skin that stretch between its front and back legs. When it jumps from a branch, it spreads its legs. The flaps of skin act like wings. The squirrel **glides** through the air to the next branch!

Snakes outgrow their skin once every few months. The old skin breaks open. Then the snake wriggles out with a shiny new skin.

Skin and fur help the animal **survive** in the place where it lives. Each animal's skin and fur can help it stay alive in some way.

This snake is wriggling out of its old skin. Snakes shed their skin a few times a year.

Glossary

camouflage – coloring that makes an animal hard to see against the plants, soil, and rocks where it lives

clear – having no color of its own, so that it can be seen through, like a window or clean water

enemy – one who wants to hurt a living thing

glides – sails or floats on air or water

protect – to keep safe

quills – long, needle-like hairs on porcupines

seasons – the different times of the year–summer, spring, winter, and fall

spines – hard, sharp, needle-like thorns or stiff hairs that protect many animals and plants

survive – live

thick – not thin; made up of closely packed things, such as hairs, feathers, or wool threads

For More Information

Books

Animal Defenses: How Animals Protect Themselves. Etta Kaner.
  (Kids Can Press)

Animal Skins & Scales. Look Once, Look Again (series).
  David M. Schwartz. (Gareth Stevens)

Chameleons And Other Animals With Amazing Skin. Scholastic News
  Nonfiction Readers (series). Susan Labella. (Children's Press)

Claws, Coats, and Camouflage. Susan E. Goodman. (Millbrook)

Web Sites

Animals on Defense

oncampus.richmond.edu/academics/education/projects/webunits/adaptations/
Learn more about different ways animals protect themselves.

Camouflage Field Book

www.harcourtschool.com/activity/camouflage/camouflage.html
Click on the animals that can hide in each place.

Index

About the Author

Jonatha A. Brown has written many nonfiction books for children. She lives in Phoenix, Arizona, with her husband, Warren, and their two dogs, Sasha and Ava. Jonatha also has two horses, Fleetwood and Freedom. She would have more animals if Warren would only let her! They both enjoy watching coyotes, rabbits, ground squirrels, lizards, and birds in their backyard.